Father to Daughter

Father to Daughter

Life Lessons on Raising a Girl

by Harry H. Harrison, Jr.

Workman Publishing Company

New York

Library of Congress Cataloging-in-Publication Data

Harrison, Harry H.

Father to daughter : life lessons on raising a girl / by Harry H. Harrison, Jr.

p. cm.

ISBN-13: 978-0-7611-2977-6; ISBN-10: 0-7611-2977-4 (alk. paper)

1. Fathers and daughters. 2. Parenting. 3. Fatherhood. I. Title.

HQ755.85 .H374 2003

306.874'2—dc21   2002038097

Workman books are available at special discounts when purchased in bulk for premiums and sales promotions as well as for fund-raising or educational use. Special editions or book excerpts can be created to specification. For details, contact the Special Sales Director at the address below.

Workman Publishing Company, Inc.

225 Varick Street

New York, NY 10014-4381

www.workman.com

Cover and book design by Paul Gamarello

Illustrations by Matt Wawiorka

Cover photograph by Julie Gang

First printing March 2003

20 19

Preface

I was amazed and gratified by the response to my earlier book, *Father to Son*. So many dads (and moms) of boys told me how much reading it meant to them. As an author, you treasure those moments.

But the most surprising thing was that dads of girls told me they read the book too. I asked them, "Well, is raising a girl like raising a boy?," and mostly they'd smile and say, "No, it's another world."

And they'd ask why there wasn't a father book for them. With all the interest and sentiment devoted to the mother-daughter relationship, the father-daughter relationship was barely even talked about. But, of course, a strong, loving father is as important to a girl as it is to a boy.

So, spurred to action by several dear friends, I set out to interview dads of successful daughters. Their daughters are academic powerhouses, star athletes, talented artists, honors graduates. These women embrace their roles as sisters and wives and friends and—especially—as daughters. These dads had obviously done an outstanding job. Their daughters will change society. Their daughters had changed their dads.

All the men I interviewed shared one precept; that it was important to be involved in their daughters' lives.

This is really their book. I just wrote down what they said.

—Harry Harrison

Raising a girl takes two parents:

A mom to show her how to be a woman.

A dad to show her how to be independent.

A dad's job is to make his daughter courageous.
Fearless. To make her feel beautiful. To give
her a sense of adventure. To make her feel secure
and confident.

The relationship between a dad and a daughter is
very simple: She will love her father and trust
him completely, forever.

Because he's her first love. Her first hero. The first
man in her life.

The Five Keys

1. Always be involved in her life.
2. Respect and honor her mom.
3. Treasure every moment with her.
4. Pray for her every day.
5. Be her hero.

The Wonder
Years

Realize from the beginning that even at one week old, she's a girl. So she's going to be just as charming, and just as mystifying, as every other girl you know. Being her dad will not change this.

Accept the fact that
she will melt your heart
anytime she chooses.

Take part in her life now. Don't wait until she's 15 to try and develop a relationship.

She may look adorable,
but be forewarned—her diaper
is going to be just as challenging
as any boy's.

When you get home from work,
hold her as much as possible.
This is for your benefit
as much as hers.

Sing to her while you're rocking her. She'll love hearing your voice—and it's a great way to pass the time at 1 A.M.

Be sure to take a lot of photos of her now. She is changing every day.

Tell her from day one
that she can accomplish
anything.

Let her sleep on your chest when she's a baby. This is when the world begins to make sense.

Yes, she's a girl. But her screams will be as loud as any baby boy's when she's hungry or tired or upset.

Make her part of your world—
let her see you shave, work,
read, and relax. She'll love
spending time with you,
no matter what you're doing.
Enjoy it while it lasts.

Memorize her face.
Her eyes. Her hands.
She'll be memorizing
everything about you.

Keep saying "Daddy" over and over to her. There's a good chance "Da-Da" will be her first word.

Introduce her to the joys
of ice cream and chocolate sauce.
She'll have as much fun playing
with it as eating it.

Give her baths.
Do not leave
this to Mom alone.
It is pure magic.

Come to grips with the fact that you cannot carry her around all her life. She will eventually have to learn to walk.

.

Remember, if you yell at a boy not to play with a wall socket, he'll either stomp off or do it anyway. A girl will cry.

When she babbles at you
in baby talk, always respond
with a positive: "Yes."
"Of course." "You're right."
Soon enough, you'll be telling
her "No" all the time.

Her mom will show her how
to bake chocolate chip cookies.
You show her how to
dunk them in milk.

Realize when she starts walking that anything she can reach will disappear. Find a childproof place for your keys. Your wallet. The TV remote.

Know that while you will never understand her thing for dolls, you will buy her more of them than you can possibly imagine.

Teach her to count.
First her fingers.
Then Cheerios, M&Ms,
dandelions, and fireflies.

Emotionally, physically,
and spiritually healthy girls
are raised in a loving atmosphere.
Do all you can to create
a tranquil, harmonious home.

Let the family dog sit under
her high chair at dinner.
Your daughter will be a source
of food for him, and the dog
will be a constant source
of wonder for her.

Invest money
in a college fund.
Now.

Be prepared to watch
Walt Disney movies with
her some 200 times.
Each.

Your wife can play Mozart
and Beethoven symphonies.
You introduce her to the Beatles.

Tickle her, play with her,
give her piggyback rides.
She's not breakable.

Never lose the wonder
of watching her and
her mother together.

Relish the moments when she toddles up and for no reason at all throws her arms around your neck. Resist the urge to buy her the world.

Trust her mom to understand the mystery of little girls. You have yet to figure out the mystery of big ones.

Realize that if you take her on a plane trip before she can talk, there's a good chance she'll scream for two and a half hours.

Encourage her
to go barefoot.

Never, ever,
make fun of her.

Bear in mind that from
the very beginning your
personality will shape her.

Realize that as you shape
her, she will shape you.

Don't think that because she's a sweet little girl she can't throw food with the best of them.

Buy her a beautiful
necklace very early on.
Continue to add links to
it as she grows older.

When you take her to the movies, be ready for her to bring along five or six of her favorite stuffed animals. When fathers of boys look at you strangely, act as if her behavior makes perfect sense.

She will want a pet.
She will also want to dress
her pet in costumes and take it
for strolls in her doll carriage.

Take her out shopping, just the two of you. But resist the urge to buy out the store.

Always remember,
she can do anything
a boy can do.

Brush her hair
occasionally. You'll be
amazed at how long she'll
want you to do this.

Never forget
that supportive fathers
produce daughters with
high self-esteem.

Read to her often.
Very soon, she'll be
reading to you.

Build a shelf for her dolls and stuffed animal collection. Ask her to tell you stories about each one.

Give her a picture of you to put in her first purse. If you're lucky, she'll always carry a photo of you.

Have tea parties with her.
Nibble on whatever she
puts in front of you.
Tell her it's delicious.

Take her to the zoo. She'll love the elephants, the monkeys, the lions, the petting zoo, everything.

Buy her a jungle gym.
However, if she falls off that
jungle gym, disregard those
thoughts about killing yourself.

Encourage her to play
with the boys.

Take her fishing.
She'll be disgusted by the worm
and the hook, but she'll love
reeling in the fish.

Play catch with her.
Even if the ball is pink
and covered with glitter.

Talk to her about what she wants to be when she grows up. Continually reinforce the idea that anything is possible.

Don't tolerate her temper tantrums. Not now. Not when she's 15. Your home will be more peaceful for this.

Restrict her TV viewing, unless you want her to grow up with the values Hollywood teaches.

Dance with her always.
She'll never be too young.
Or old.

Remember, if little girls don't get a nap, they can resemble something from a Stephen King novel.

Put her in galoshes and take her out to stomp in mud puddles.

Little girls are fascinated
by escalators. Make sure
you hold hands.

Make her
a Valentine's Day card—
every year.

Take her horseback riding.
Girls *love* horses.

Lie on your backs in the grass together and look for shapes in the clouds. It's a good way to approach life when you're young.

You'll notice that little girls
love to have their faces painted.
So do bigger girls,
only they use makeup.

Be home for
dinner on time.
Very important.

Believe it or not, when she's two and a half, she's ready for a bike with training wheels. You, however, might not be.

Buy her cycling gloves and
a helmet when you're ready
to take the training wheels off.
It saves a lot of scraped
skin and tears.

Ask her about her day,
every day.
Share her wonder.

Keep her secrets.
This way she will begin
to trust men.

Write this down:
Girls cry. A lot.

Sure, give her a baseball glove for her birthday.

Young girls love a hose and a sandbox. They also love to rip off their clothes after they get them wet. Don't freak out.

Take her for a walk
in the woods. Show her what
poison ivy looks like,
how to cross a stream,
how to find her way back.

Let her teach you.
About what she learned in
school today. About the Pilgrims,
or multiplication, or manatees.
How to sing her favorite song.
How to bake a cake.
How to braid Barbie's hair.

Show her how
to play poker.

Resist the urge to let her sleep
in your bed when she's scared
or sick. Independence starts in
childhood. Instead, sit with her
in her own room until she falls
back to sleep.

Teach her not to be
afraid of boys, but to be
ready to challenge them.

When she's old enough, sign her up for karate lessons. This is more for your sake than hers.

Plant flowers with her.
Even if your garden
is on a windowsill.

Don't be surprised if,
on her first sleepover,
she calls you at 3 A.M. to come
pick her up. The fact that she
misses you is a wonderful thing.

She will fall in love
with dogs, kittens, birds,
and stuffed unicorns.
It may make no sense to you.
Just smile.

If another girl or boy hurts her in any way, you will have the very real inclination to inflict harm. Resist it. This impulse won't get any weaker as your daughter gets older.

Show her how to
climb up a tree.
Also, how to climb down.

Praise her often. Let her know
you love her the way she is.
If you tell her this often enough
she might remember it throughout
adolescence.

Make up stories
to tell each other at night.
Stretch her imagination.

Remember, little sisters will idolize, chase, and annoy their big brothers and sisters all through their teenage years. It's really no one's fault.

Teach her how and when to call 911.

This cannot be said enough:
Don't give in to the urge
to buy her everything.
(You'll bankrupt the family.)

Learn to read her moods.
The day is coming when she won't
talk about everything with you.

Buy her a chemistry set.

Get involved in her school.
Go to the PTA meetings.
Meet her teachers.
Know what's going on.

Encourage her to try new things while she's young, and she'll be more willing to try new things when she is older.

Teach her to take pride in who she is.

Surprise her by showing up
at her school for lunch,
bearing Happy Meals or pizza.

Always respect
her privacy.
And modesty.

Don't pry into the stories she and her mother tell each other. They'll let you in on them when they want to.

Read her stories from the newspaper. This will spark a lifelong habit.

The earlier you buy her a computer, the sooner using it will become second nature.

Reinforce her interest in math and science, both inside and outside the classroom.

Show her how to throw a right cross. That will stop any boy from picking on her.

Talk to her about drugs
and alcohol early and often.
You don't want her to learn
this stuff from anybody else.

Never argue with her
mom in front of her.
As hard as it may be,
walk away.

Encourage her to trust her instincts, especially when a person or a place feels unsafe.

Remember, society is teaching
her its values 24/7.
You need to be more determined
to teach her yours.

Insist that she not wear
makeup until she's
in middle school.

Never permit her to talk back rudely—to you or to her mother. Or anybody else, for that matter.

Teach her patience,
kindness, and tolerance.
If you don't, many years
from now you'll wish you had.

Display her artwork in your office. Why should all the good stuff go on the refrigerator?

Take her to the golf course with you. Give her a sawed-off club she can use to whack balls around.

Encourage her to
compliment others.

Eat breakfast with her.
This will give her
a reason to be
at the table on time.

Think before you speak.
Even when you don't
mean to, you can end up
hurting her feelings.

Teach her that her actions speak louder than her words. Even if she's screaming her words.

Never laugh
at her dreams.

Impress upon her the three R's:
Respect for self.
Respect for others.
Responsibility for all her actions.

Remind her to correct
a mistake as soon as she
realizes she's made one.

Encourage her to spend
time by herself.

Teach her to read between
the lines. Remember, though,
that she will probably have
a better natural ability
for this than you.

Share your knowledge
with her.

Never let her forget that you love her. Even when you're angry with her.

Remind her never
to interrupt when
she's being flattered.

Take her out of town to somewhere she's never been at least once a year. This will develop her sense of adventure.

Don't miss a recital, concert, play, or any other performance of hers. Not now. Not until she graduates.

Encourage her to be kind.
Even to the girl nobody likes.

Make sure she can reach
you 24 hours a day.

Tell her
when you're wrong.
And apologize.

Remember, she needs a strong self-image *before* she becomes an awkward teen. A father's love can make all the difference.

The Mystery
Years

Accept the fact that the loving, tender angel you've spent the last decade with may disappear sometimes. She will return.

Remember,
teenage girls spend hours
in their room doing something.
No man has ever really figured
out what that something is.

Sometimes (okay, many times),
she may not know what she wants.
Your job is to help her
figure it out.

Once she begins
to develop physically
and sexually,
don't pull away from her.

Insist she go to bed
at a reasonable hour.
Teenage girls need more
sleep than babies do.

Resist installing a phone
in her room, no matter how
much she begs for one.
She will be up all night with it.

Throw away the scales
(weight gain during puberty
is normal). Stress healthy eating,
exercise, and plenty of sleep.

Tell her she looks
beautiful in braces.
Show her a photo of what
you looked like in yours.

Get to know all her friends. Middle school marks the zenith of peer influence.

Remember that the rules have changed. Girls today excel at soccer, math, baseball, computers, politics, swimming, engineering. . . . Don't hold her back.

Remind her that
the most sacred thing
between a father and
daughter is trust.

Drive the car pool.
You'll learn firsthand
what she's doing
each day.

Remember, when she's 13, she's heard all about sex, drugs, violence, alcohol, and guns from television, magazines, movies, and friends. Hopefully she's already learned about them from you.

Spend time together
as a family.

Remember, when you're dealing with a 13-year-old girl, for all intents and purposes you're dealing with a fruitcake.

Listen to the music
she's listening to
(and don't forget what your
parents thought of what you
listened to).

Talk to her often about
decision-making and sex.
About peer pressure, about love,
about romance, about God.
You never know when it will be
just the thing she needs to hear.

Teach her that gossiping will eat at her soul.

Never undervalue
her intelligence.

Watch your language
around her.
Insist she watch hers.

Be prepared to hear her say that she hates her mother. Be firm and insistent about the need for respect.

Give her household chores to accomplish and hold her accountable. These will help her keep in touch with family life.

Teach her not to judge
other people by the labels
they wear.

Review her homework with her nightly and drill her to help study for tests. This is an outstanding way to spend time with her.

Girls this age can be uncomfortable stating what they really need. More often than not, she needs you to be a parent.

Adolescent girls congregate in shopping malls. Drive her there. Make sure she knows, and you know, who's bringing her home.

Don't put any more restrictions on your daughter than you would on a son at the same age and maturity level.

Accept the fact that girls squeal when they're happy or confused or excited or scared or because they just saw a certain boy in line.

Teach her that there's nothing she can't accomplish.

Tell her to believe
in true love,
just not in junior high.

When she's particularly angry, sit down with her and have her try to describe what's going on. Remember, the longer you listen, the more you'll learn.

Monitor her TV and movies.
Or else she just might believe
she should be sexually active,
dangerously thin, experimenting
with drugs, and hanging out with
rock stars.

Remember that most big sisters lord it over their little brothers. Remember, also, that most little brothers have ways of getting even.

Don't subscribe to magazines that exploit women. It makes a statement about how you view all women.

Play tennis or some other sport with her once a week. Even if you're a terrible player, it's a great way to spend time with her.

When it comes to e-mail,
Web sites, and on-line chat rooms,
make sure she is able to recognize
and avoid dangerous or
inappropriate possibilities.

If you don't approve of the way she looks before she goes out, send her back to her room to start over. Be gentle but firm.

There will be days when you think you've raised an alien. Those are the same days she feels she's being raised by one.

No body piercing below her ears—this is where a dad must take a stand.

The most stressful thing about her first school dance will be fitting a dozen girls into your car.

Girls can be emotional
roller coasters and dads tend
to be emotionally distant.
She's part of your life; let it show.

Don't let her play
you and her mother
against each other.

There will be days where nothing you say to her is right. That's okay. You're the adult. Say what you feel needs to be said.

When she's looking at the fashion models in a magazine, it's a good time to discuss airbrushing, advertising, and techniques of persuasion.

Never call her names.
No matter how mad you are.
No matter what she did.
If you do, she'll remember it
for the rest of her life.

Remember—many girls
look back on middle school
as the worst time in their lives.
Stay tuned; stay involved.

Teach her to call if she's going to be five minutes late or if she's changing locations. Always.

Be the one who takes her to her first rock concert. Take earplugs, though. You probably don't remember how loud they are.

Teach her to
read the instructions.

Keep in mind they only teach sex "education" in schools. It's your job to teach sex "decision-making."

Volunteer to drive her and her friends to the movies. Then just listen while they talk.

Don't hesitate to call the parents
of her friends if you know
or suspect alcohol,
drug use, or sexual activity.
You would want to be informed if
those parents were in your shoes.

Never tell sexist jokes. They will come back to haunt you.

Teach her to think
before she speaks
(and practice what you preach).

Impress upon her that there
are direct correlations between
studying and good grades,
good grades and college,
college and success.

Help her discover what she's passionate about, then help her pursue it.

Learn who her role models are.
If they are just pop stars
and fashion models,
you have some work to do.

Face it—boys are now indispensable to her.

Understand that it's possible
for a girl who has everything
to be miserable sometimes.
Remember, you can't always
fix all her problems.

She may decide
to punish you
by not talking.
Enjoy the peace.

There will be times when
she will knock you over
with her selflessness,
tenderness, and gentleness.
This is the real her.

Girls & Spirituality

The day she's born,
ask God to guide you in
all aspects of raising her.

Talk about spiritual matters at
the dinner table as much as you
talk about sports or politics or
her allowance.

Drag her to church or temple every week. She may not share your enthusiasm, but after 18 years, the message will have sunk in.

Forgive her when she seeks forgiveness. This is the best way for her to learn to forgive others.

Write her a short poem
that includes her name
and how much you and
her mother and God love her.
Recite it to her every night
at prayer time.

Explain to her that God doesn't speak in code. She can figure out what He wants if she just stays in contact with Him.

Teach her how to be moral in an age that bombards her with sexual imagery and innuendo.

Encourage her to join the youth group at her church or temple.

Stress to her that
one key to happiness
is never to take
anything personally.

Ask her every now and then about her spiritual life. If she asks you what you mean, be prepared to have a discussion with her.

Counsel her to look deep inside herself when she's searching for the answer to a difficult problem.

Teach her to pray
for her enemies.
This could possibly
include a rotating cast of
classmates and ex-boyfriends.

Teach her to treat each day as holy.

Encourage her to
look for the good in
everybody, but to beware
of evil in the world.

Convince her that
self-pity is a waste of time.

Help her understand
that there's more
to life than wearing
the right jeans.

Teach her that sometimes
God has other plans.

Girls & Sports

Don't be the dad who takes his daughter's sports too seriously. You'll miss some great times.

Sign her up for a variety of
sports when she's little.
After a couple of seasons,
let her decide for herself
which ones she'd like to continue.

Her first soccer team may be called the Pansies. You may have to wear a T-shirt with pansies all over it. There are worse things.

Keep in mind that little girls
are not always chasing the ball.
They're often running simply
because everyone else is running.

Reassure her that she
will be okay if she gets hurt.
(Reassure her mother of this, too.)

When she's young, chances are she'll be better at sports than most boys. Don't let this go to your head. It's not genetics; it's child development.

The first rule
to lay down:
Grades always come first.

Practice basketball, softball,
or soccer with her when
you get home from work.
She'll love playing with you.
She might even beat you.

Teach her how to throw
a curve ball . . . and how
to handle the curve balls
life will throw at her.

Take her to college
or professional women's
sporting events. These athletes are
real inspirations for young girls.

Go jogging with her.
Start when she's young,
so when she gets faster than you,
she'll still invite you to join her.

Yes, girls today
play hockey.
They can clean
your clock.

Don't think buying her soccer cleats is going to be any easier (or cheaper) than buying her other shoes.

Send her to sports camp.

Don't forget, competitive girls' sports are no more played by young ladies than competitive boys' sports are played by young gentlemen. It's rough out there.

Be prepared
to be amazed by
her accomplishments.

No matter how much you are tempted, don't yell at the refs or insult the umpire. You'll embarrass her and look like an idiot.

Deal with the fact that if she's 16
and still participating,
you can't coach her.
She's better than you will ever be.

Accept the fact that she just may be terrible. A lot of gifted musicians and mathematicians couldn't hit a house with a ball from five feet.

You may feel the urge to paint your stomach and face with her team's colors. Resist it.

Don't think that a boy is the only thing that can break her heart. Losing a game can, too.

You may need to remind yourself
that the other team isn't bigger.
The other team isn't older.
The other team wasn't just
released from women's prison.

Remember, athletics enhance
a girl's self-esteem,
increase confidence, and
improve scholastic performance.
As if she needed an excuse.

Show her how
to lose with dignity.

Teach her how
to win gracefully.

Girls & Money

Teach her that money cannot solve all ills.

Give her a piggy bank
when she's little.
She's never too young to
learn the value of saving.

Provide her with opportunities to earn money, starting at an early age. Even a young child can clean her room, help sort and fold laundry, and water plants.

Send her on simple errands to
the grocery store or drugstore,
so she becomes comfortable
handling money and learns
the cost of basic items.

Give her
a regular allowance.
Raises and bonuses
are possible,
but should be earned.

Encourage her
to save some of her
birthday money.

She'll say she wants a purse that's more expensive than her mother's. Impress upon her that there's honor in a hard day's work. And money.

Learn to say,
"We can't afford it."

Show her how much to tip—and when.

Teach her not to
buy anything with
a credit card that she
can't pay off that month.

Show her how to save
money. Start by letting
her watch you save.

Warn her about debt.

Teach her how to negotiate.

Help her to find a good job.

If necessary,
remind her that whining,
crying, and begging
won't gain her access
to her father's wallet.

Show her how to read
the financial page.

Teach her to take her job seriously, no matter what the job.

Discuss real-world costs.
Apartment rents and utility bills
can come as a real shock
once she leaves the nest.

Explain to her that the greatest satisfaction of wealth is putting it to work to help others.

Girls & Cars

You will have to teach her how to drive . . . without making her cry.

Let her drive you around.
Sit there, look out the window,
and do not criticize her.
This is how she'll gain confidence.

Realize her automobile insurance will be the price of a boat.

Make it very clear that you expect her to wear a seat belt. Even over her prom dress.

Show her how to change a tire. She'll still call you at 1 A.M., but one night, you might not be there.

Make sure she learns how to drive in the rain, in the snow, and on icy roads. Stay at it until she can drive in these conditions with confidence.

Get her an AAA card, and make sure she always carries it with her.

Have a spare pair of car keys made if getting anywhere on time is important to you and your wife.

Before she sets off in a car by herself, remind her that her eyes must always be on the road, even when the CD has ended or her least favorite song comes on the radio.

When she's a new driver, place a limit on the number of friends who are allowed in the car at one time.

Show her how to read a road map.

Take a defensive driving class together. You'll both learn some valuable information about driving safely.

Don't buy the idea that
just because she's a she,
she's automatically
a safe driver.

Remind yourself—
and your daughter—
that no teenager
needs a brand new car.

Keep in mind that with her first car, the object is to surround her with the biggest, strongest tank you can afford. While society might not sleep better because of this, you will.

Give her a cell phone
for emergencies only.
Agree upon what an emergency is.
She may think it's when
she hasn't talked to her boyfriend
in the last 30 minutes.

Persuade her to buy gas when the fuel tank level is at a quarter tank, not when the needle is buried and the car is riding on fumes.

Lay down strict laws about
drinking and driving.
Don't hesitate to enforce them.

Teach her that the most important thing to look for in a car is that it starts every morning.

Girls & Boys

Odd-looking boys will start
showing up at your house.
This is to be expected because
adolescent boys are odd-looking.

Let her see,
by the way you treat your wife,
the way a man is supposed to
treat a woman.

Tell her not to judge men by their looks or money.

Teach her how to look
a boy in the eye and say
"No."

Do not tease her
about boyfriends.
She may not have one,
and you might make her feel
like she's supposed to.

Chaperone
a school dance.
You'll learn a lot
about the boys in her life.

Understand that if she suddenly becomes a football fanatic even though she hates the game, you can be sure a boy is involved.

Teach her that if she acts stupid to attract boys, she'll attract stupid boys.

Don't assume that every boy that shows up at your house is a threat to your daughter's virginity. He might just be her ticket to passing history.

Explain to her that there
are dangerous boys
as well as honorable ones,
and how to tell the difference.

If a boy pulls up and honks for her, go out and have words with him. Explain that your daughter answers to a doorbell.

Remember, it's a good thing if the boys in her life think you are slightly unstable.

Tell her not to be overwhelmed just because an upperclassman asks her out.

Do not follow her
on her first car date.
(You'll be tempted.)

Remind yourself that
the Martians who show up at
your front door looking for your
daughter actually have parents.

Ask her and her date what their plans for the night are. If you don't like the plans, help them make new ones. Your daughter will hate this. It doesn't matter.

Make sure the evening ends
with the boy bringing her home,
not taking her to another girl's
house. Unless you really know
and trust that family. And the boy.

Assure her that her first boyfriend won't be her last. And to make decisions accordingly.

Know that she will not like it if you become better friends with her boyfriend than she is.

Wait up for her. Knowing Dad will be greeting her at the door has a very positive effect on her decision-making process.

Remember, every girl's heart gets broken. There's nothing you can do to fix it. Hunting down the boy won't help. On the other hand, she will also break a few hearts herself.

Understand that talking with your daughter about sex will be some of the hardest conversations ever. Keep in mind that they will also be some of the most important conversations you have.

If she starts moping at meals and barking at her family and if she refuses to talk to one certain boy, you can be sure she's making his life miserable as well.

Teach her to never confuse abuse with love. Violent behavior does *not* mean that he cares.

Stress that she's not to get into a car with a drunk, no matter how much she "loves" him. Tell her to call you.

Make sure she knows she can call you at any time and you will go get her. This is why the cell phone was invented.

Don't get too
emotionally involved
in her love life.
It will drive you nuts.

Older Girls

Hug her before bedtime
every night. Even when she's 18.
It's important to remember
what really matters.

Never forget,
your influence is huge.
The way you lead your life has a
direct impact upon how successful
she becomes in her own life.

Help her set goals.
If she has nothing to aim for,
what will she shoot for?

During those rare times when
she actually wants to talk to you,
turn the TV off and listen.
You never know when
this will happen again.

Show her how to shake hands firmly.

Don't let her moods
or anger push you away.
She needs you now
more than ever.

You have no power over how much makeup, shampoo, suntan lotion, skin creams, hair color treatment, mascara, eyeliner, perfume, cologne, body wash, and bath lotion she will buy. Accept this and move on.

Assure her that she's a knockout. But remind her of all her other fabulous qualities, too.

Encourage her to compete—
to run for the student council,
to try out for the varsity team,
to put something on the line.

Competition for the school play, for academic bowl, or for student government can be absolutely ferocious, and losing will always be difficult and painful. If she doesn't succeed, comfort her but make sure she tries again.

Talk to her often
about college.
About graduate school.
About careers.
About her dreams.

Be firm about maintaining family traditions. They will become more important to her than either of you can imagine.

When you're upset with her, don't bring up ancient history. Concentrate on the here and now.

Learn her language. When she says a date was "fine" or "okay," what is she really saying?

Remember, fashion models
are thinner than 98 percent
of American women and girls.
Do not let her believe she can diet
and exercise her way to this look.

Stay out of the fights
between her and her mother,
unless you judge one or both
as being completely irrational.
Then venture in at your own risk.

Take long walks with her.
If you just listen,
she'll eventually tell you
everything that's on her mind.

Teach her not to take people for granted.

Set down a strict curfew every year, based on her age and maturity. Resign yourself to the fact that she will always complain about it—right up to college.

Never criticize her
in front of her friends.

Teach her to avoid reckless people.

Make sure she joins clubs or school organizations. She may say it's a waste of time and that none of her friends are doing it. But she'll get to know other goal-oriented kids (plus, it will look great on her college applications).

Remember, if her home life is crazy, the rest of her life will be too.

Teach her
to respect herself.

Don't let her miss school to get her hair done for a party. Unless all you want is a party girl.

Remember, you're her definition of a man. If you drink and smoke and take drugs, chances are the men in her life will, too.

She'll say you're always lecturing her; you'll say she never listens. You will both be right.

Help her to become independent from you.

If she's embarrassed because of your car or her car or her house, she has some more growing up to do.

Encourage her to volunteer.
A great cure for a selfish teen
is community work.

Teach her
to take the lead.

She will decide you need
a complete, head-to-toe,
fashion makeover. Beware!
This will not make you look cool.

Let her make mistakes.

Show her that
excuses aren't necessary.

Understand that when she's 15,
and wearing a black dress,
with her hair done and face
made up, you will be very hesitant
to let her leave the house.

Realize that you can't be everything to her.

Point out to her that achievement seems to follow those who start early and work late.

When it comes to parties, there's no such thing as too much information. Call the parents and find out if they'll be present. If you suspect alcohol will be served, don't let her attend.

Don't think you've reached the perfect compromise by letting her and her friends drink in your home. All you're doing is teaching her to drink.

Help her learn to be comfortable with silence.

One day she will ask
you questions about
birth control and abortion.
Be prepared to answer them.
But don't assume anything.

Teach her that jealousy serves no purpose but to make you feel bad.

Remind her, continually, that she has the power to change the world.

Encourage her
to be happy for other
people's successes.

Visit college campuses with her in her junior year. (This is not the time to get emotional. There will be plenty of time for that.)

Even when she's a high school senior, always know where she's going each night and where she's been the night before.

Remember to let her face the consequences of her own actions. They are the best teachers. She doesn't learn anything if she's caught cheating or stealing and you come to her rescue.

Teach her to stand up
for her decisions.
And to be willing
to change her mind.

There will be times when you'd rather stick needles in your eyes than have a particular conversation with her. This is when you must act like a father.

Prepare for the day
when you're not
the most important man
in her life.

Convince her not to be
paralyzed by fear.
Or fear of failure.

Help her identify
the colleges she wants to attend.
Start applying the first semester
of her senior year.

Don't let her choose
a college because that's
where her boyfriend
is going.

Believe in her.

You'll notice that toward the end of her last semester of high school, her evenings will get started about the time you're tossing down your Metamucil.

Take her out to dinner,
just the two of you.

Tell her the three keys to wisdom:
not believing all you hear,
not spending all you have,
not sleeping all you want.
This will be difficult for her until
she graduates from college.

Teach her that great love
and great achievements
involve great risk.

Compromise.

Let her know that true happiness comes from within.

Explain to her
that not getting what
you want is sometimes
a stroke of luck.

Remind her that her character is her destiny.

Caution her against
working *too* hard.

Teach her not to hold on
to anything too tightly.

Explain to her that failure
is an integral part of success,
and that she must keep trying.

Inspire her
to never give up.

Have a look around her room.
Take a moment to look at
her pictures, her photos,
her keepsakes.
These are her memories.
This was the childhood
you gave her.

Remember, she will break your heart when she leaves for college. But you will survive.

Tell her she is the daughter you always dreamed about.